CU00839365

Crazy Presents

Crazy Presents

Juliet Bawden

Designed by Jane Laycock
Illustrated by Jane Laycock and Shelagh McGee

HUTCHINSON
London Sydney Auckland Johannesburg

For Jill Sheridan, and John and
Sasha Haworth with love

First published in Great Britain in 1989 by Hutchinson Children's Books
An imprint of Century Hutchinson Ltd
Brookmount House, 62–65 Chandos Place, Covent Garden,
London WC2N 4NW

Century Hutchinson Australia (Pty) Ltd
20 Alfred Street, Milsons Point, Sydney 2061, Australia

Century Hutchinson New Zealand Limited
32–34 View Road, PO Box 40–086, Glenfield, Auckland 10

Century Hutchinson South Africa (Pty) Ltd
PO Box 337, Bergvlei 2012, South Africa

Set in Times
by JH Graphics Ltd, Reading

Printed and bound in Great Britain by
Courier International Ltd, Tiptree, Essex

British Library Cataloguing in Publication Data

Bawden, Juliet
Crazy Presents
1. Handicrafts for children — Manuals
I. Title
745.5'088054

ISBN 0-09-174091-6

Contents

Introduction

Crazy presents is full of ideas for making presents that people really want. If you have enough pocket money it is easy to go out and buy a present, but a present *made* by you for someone else is very special. It shows that you have taken the time and trouble to think about the person to whom you are giving the gift.

Even famous people, such as Zandra Rhodes, the dress designer, still find time to make presents for their friends and family.

Some of the presents cost pennies to make, others are a little more expensive. You will find presents for the very young to the very old. You will find presents that make use of your particular skill, whether it be sewing, cooking or even amusing small children. And so that your presents look beautiful, I have finished with a section on gift wrapping.

The dots at the beginning of each project show how easy it is to make it. One dot means it is very easy, two dots mean it is a little more difficult and three dots mean that you will have to concentrate really hard! It is a good idea to start on the easy projects and then go on to the harder ones. If in doubt ask a grown up to help with the more difficult projects.

I hope you have lots of fun making and giving these presents!

Presents for a New Baby

Babies love bright colours, and all the presents in this section are made with brightly coloured material.

●● Mobile

One of the first things a baby does is look at things. So a lovely present for a new baby is a mobile.
Use simple shapes and follow a theme, such as the weather or different animals.

You will need

Tracing paper and pencil
Scissors (pinking shears optional)
Felt pieces in various colours and sizes
Wadding
Dressmaker's pins
Needle and cotton
Bits and pieces for decorating, eg buttons and glitter
Piece of cane *or* milliner's wire *or* fine dowelling, 70cm
    long
Glue (Copydex is ideal)
Wire cutters *or* a small saw for cutting the cane, dowell or
    milliner's wire.
Button or embroidery thread

9

Instructions

1. Trace the patterns shown here or draw your own designs.

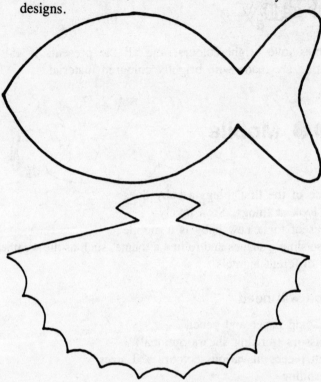

2. Add a 1cm border around the design, then cut out the tracing paper pattern.

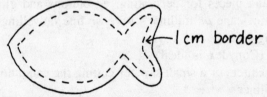

1cm border

3. Make a sandwich of two pieces of felt with a piece of

10

wadding in between. Pin the tracing paper pattern to this.

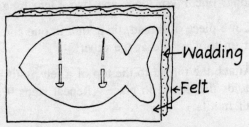

4. Using a running stitch, sew through the paper, felt and wadding, following the lines of the drawing.

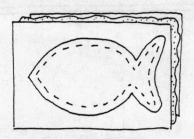

5. When you have finished, remove all the pins and pull away the tracing paper.

6. Using pinking shears or dressmaker's scissors, cut around the sewn shape. Be careful not to cut too close to the stitching line — leave about 5mm clear.

7. Stick on any decorative features, such as eyes, on your felt shape.

8. Cut the cane into four different lengths: one 25cm long, one 17cm long, and two 13cm long.

9. Cut a piece of thread, tie a knot in one end and thread it on to a needle at the other.

10. Attach the thread to the top of a felt motif so the knot holds the thread in place. (Repeat steps 9 and 10 for all motifs.)

11. Remove the needle and tie the loose end of thread on to the middle of the longest piece of cane.

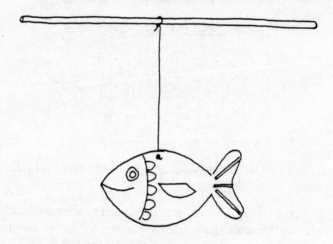

12. Tie the other motifs to the ends of the pieces of cane and hang these from the first piece of cane as shown.

13. Hang the mobile so that the longest piece of cane is at the top, followed by the middle-sized length, and finally by the two smaller pieces. You will have to adjust the lengths of thread on the motifs so that the mobile balances. You can also hang some motifs from others.

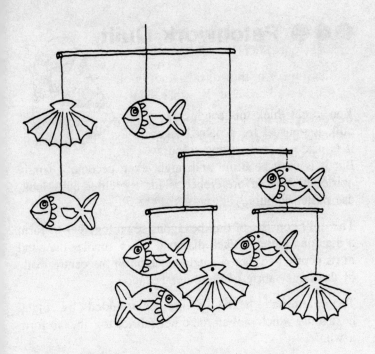

●●● Patchwork Quilt

You might think this patchwork
quilt is unusual for a baby because
it is made in such strong colours.
But it is very beautiful and might even become a family
heirloom! If your preference is for a prettier baby look,
use pastel colours.

The quilt consists of tiny hexagons sewn together to form
a diamond pattern. Each diamond has a smaller diamond
in its centre and then a single hexagon in the centre made
of the same fabric as the outer hexagon.

The patterned hexagons are surrounded by black
hexagons, which pull all the other fabrics together to form
a whole.

As the quilt is small it is important that the fabrics you
choose have small-scale patterns. Having said that,
however, fine striping from an old shirt is ideal.

You will need

Pencil
Tracing paper
Scissors
Pins
Enough fabric remnants to make:
    18 full diamond shapes (shape A)
    4 half diamond shapes (shape B)
    6 half diamond shapes (shape C)
    4 quarter diamond shapes (shapes D and E)

1.5m of background colour, in this case black, to make 370 hexagons.

Piece of wadding 75cm × 80cm

Piece of lining fabric, 75cm × 80cm. Brushed cotton is ideal; we used a red cotton.

Instructions

1. Trace a hexagon on a piece of tracing paper, and cut it out. This is your template. You will need one template for every fabric hexagon you make.

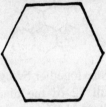

2. Pin the template to a piece of fabric and cut around it so you have a fabric hexagon that is slightly larger than the template. Fold the excess material over the sides of the template and tack it down to the paper. Repeat this for every hexagon you make.

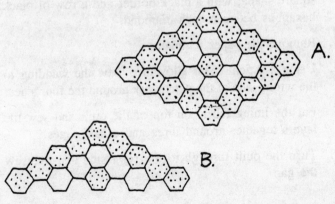

A.

B.

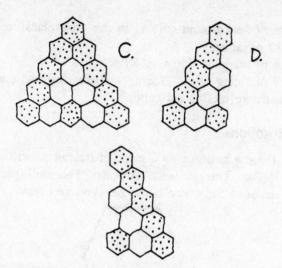

C.

D.

3. Sew your hexagons together by oversewing along each edge to make all 32 of the diamond shapes shown above. You will need 25 hexagons for one full diamond shape, 15 hexagons for a half diamond shape and 9 hexagons for a quarter diamond shape.

4. Join these diamond shapes together with black hexagons, as shown opposite, to make a large, almost square shape, with a black border and a row of black hexagons between each diamond.

5. Remove the paper templates.

6. Using a 0.5cm seam allowance, sew the wadding to the wrong side of the patchwork around the four sides.

7. Put the lining fabric on top of the quilt and sew the layers together around three and a half edges.

8. Turn the quilt through to the right side and oversew the gap.

9. Finish the quilt by sewing a line of topstitching all round the edges, about 2mm from the side.

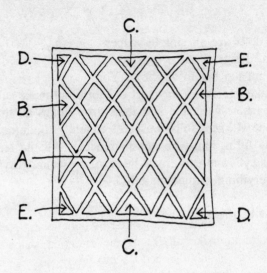

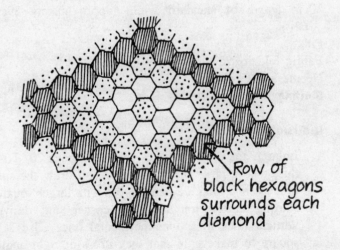

Row of black hexagons surrounds each diamond

●● First Doll

These dolls are all simple shapes and are designed to be easy to grasp but too big to swallow. You can make one out of any sort of fabric but make sure that it is machine-washable as babies drop things all the time and so it will need to be washed frequently. Both the fabric and the filling must be non-flammable. All the features, such as eyes and ears, must be sewn on securely as babies put everything in their mouths.

You will need

Pencil
Ruler
Large piece of paper
Scissors
20cm length of standard width (approximately 39cm)
    fabric
Pins
Fabric felt tips or embroidery thread
Needle and thread
Stuffing

Instructions

1. Enlarge one of the patterns shown on page 20. To do this, take a large piece of paper and draw the same grid as shown on the pattern, but with larger squares, starting at the top left-hand corner and drawing vertical lines first, then horizontal ones. Use a set square to make sure that they cross at right angles.

18

(Alternatively, you can use some dressmakers' grid paper.)

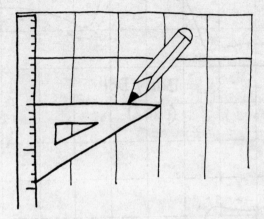

2. Copy the pattern from the original, working on one square at a time. First, mark where any lines meet within your square with a dot. Then join the dots. Copy the pattern into all the squares using the same method.

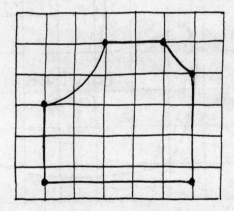

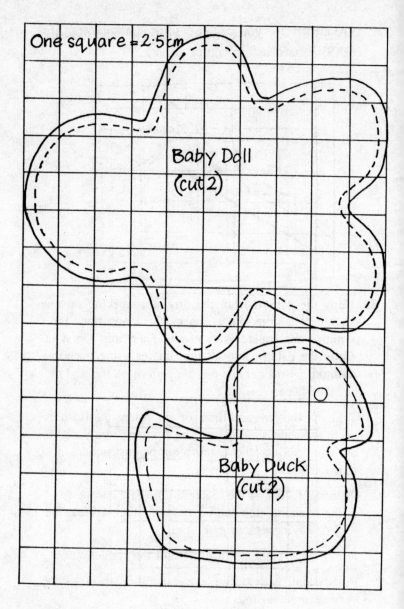

One square = 2·5 cm

Baby Doll
(cut 2)

Baby Duck
(cut 2)

3. Make sure you add seam allowances around the edge of the pattern before cutting it out.

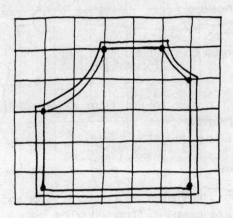

4. Fold the fabric in half, pin the pattern on top and cut out the shape.

5. Take out the pins and draw or embroider the features on to the right side of both the front and the back. If drawing, follow the manufacturer's instructions for fixing fabric.

6. With right sides of the material together, pin the front to the back and sew with a running stitch around the edges, leaving a 5cm gap.

7. Remove the pins and turn the doll the right side out.

8. Fill the doll with stuffing, oversew the gap and knot very securely to finish.

●● Nursery Coat Hanger

You will need

Piece of paper
Child's wooden coat hanger, 30cm long
Pencil
Scissors
Piece of felt in main colour, 37cm × 15cm
Needle and thread
Non-toxic fabric glue

Instructions

1. Place the coat hanger on a piece of paper and draw a pencil line around it. Then add a 1cm seam allowance around this. This is your pattern. Cut out four webbed feet motifs and two of each head piece as shown in the pattern instructions.

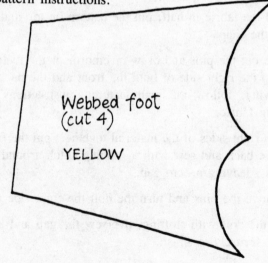

Webbed foot
(cut 4)

YELLOW

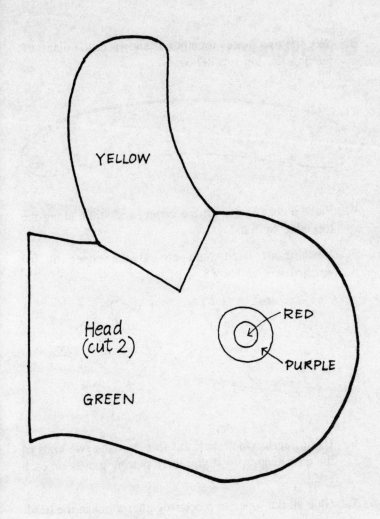

YELLOW

Head
(cut 2)

RED

PURPLE

GREEN

2. Using the coat hanger pattern, cut out two hanger shapes from felt.

3. Sew the two pieces together as shown in the diagram, leaving the top unstitched.

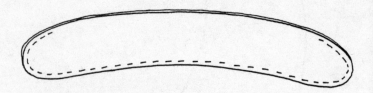

4. Place a coat hanger in the cover, and stitch along the top edge by hand.

5. Machine or hand-stitch around the edges of the webbed feet as shown.

6. Using fabric glue, stick the feet over the two ends of the coat hanger, as if you were putting gloves on each end.

7. Glue all the separate pieces together to make the head.

8. Hand-stitch or glue the two head pieces together, sandwiching the coat hanger in the middle.

By using this basic pattern, you can make a variety of different designs, such as lambs, cows, pigs, frogs, and tigers.

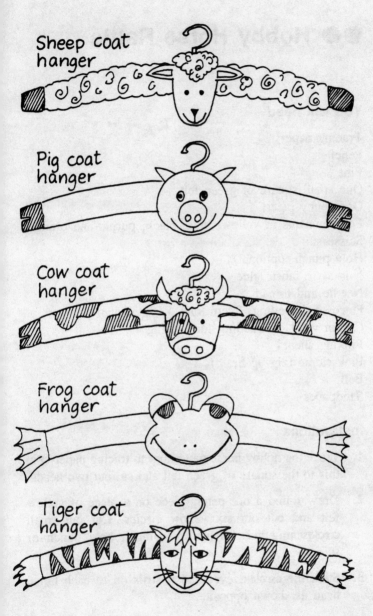

Sheep coat hanger

Pig coat hanger

Cow coat hanger

Frog coat hanger

Tiger coat hanger

25

●● Hobby Horse Rattle

You will need

Tracing paper
Pencil
Pins
One small square of green felt
One-penny piece
Felt remnants in yellow, blue, black, purple and orange
Scissors
Hole punch (optional)
Non-toxic fabric glue
Needle and thread
Piece of dowelling, 22cm long × 9mm diameter
Cotton wool or wadding for stuffing
Pinking shears
Pink ricrac (zigzag braid)
Bell
Sandpaper

Instructions

1. Trace the hobby horse pattern on to tracing paper. Pin this to the square of green felt and cut out two heads.

2. Draw round a one-penny piece on a piece of yellow felt and cut out six yellow circles. Cut out small circles in other colours by using a hole punch or scissors.

3. Stick the circles, eyes and nostrils on to each horse head as shown opposite.

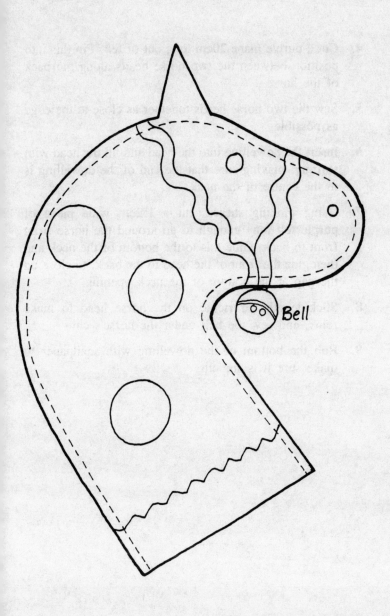

Bell

4. Cut a purple mane 20cm long out of felt. Pin this into position between the two horse heads along the back of the horse.

5. Sew the two horse heads together as close to the edge as possible.

6. Insert the dowelling into the head and fill the head with stuffing, making sure that the end of the dowelling is in the centre of the neck.

7. Using pinking shears, cut a 1.2cm wide piece of purple felt long enough to go around the horse from front to back. Glue this to the bottom of the neck and then glue the front of the head to the back, to close up the gap at the bottom of the neck opening.

8. Stick lengths of ricrac on the horse head to make reins, and sew the bell under the horse's chin.

9. Rub the bottom of the dowelling with sandpaper to make sure it is smooth.

●● Patchwork Clown

Although this clown is not made
from patchwork he is made from
fabric remnants. He is cheap and
easy to make, and small children will love him. Make sure
everything is sewn on very securely and that all materials
used are safe!

You will need

Piece of cardboard
Scissors
Pen
Pieces of brightly coloured fabric, large enough to cut out
    circles of the following diameters: 12cm, 14cm, 20cm
    or approximately 2.8m of 90cm wide cotton
Needle and thread
20cm of knitted cotton for the face (part of an old white
    or cream T-shirt would do)
20cm of cotton fabric for the hands and feet
Kapok or cotton wool *or* old tights for stuffing
86cm of cord elastic
Felt *or* embroidery thread
Double knitting wool *or* wool fringing
2 bells

Instructions

1. Cut three circles out of card with the following
   diameters: 12cm, 14cm, and 20cm.

2. Use the circles as patterns and draw round them on to

the back of your fabric. Draw and cut out 36 arm circles with a 12cm diameter, 40 leg circles with a diameter of 14cm, and 18 body circles with a diameter of 20cm.

3. Fold the fabric circles into quarters and cut a hole in the centre of each.

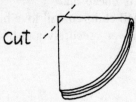

4. Sew a line of running stitches round the edge of each circle.

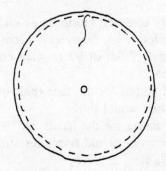

5. Gather up the circle by pulling the stitches tight and secure the cotton with a knot.

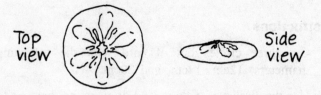

6. Cut out two head shapes, four feet shapes and four hand shapes as shown below and on page 32. Make two pairs of hands and feet and one head. With the right sides together, sew the fronts to the backs as close to the edge as possible, leaving a gap at the neck, wrist and ankle.

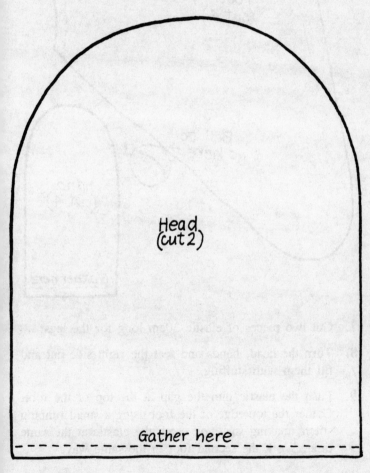

Head
(cut 2)

Gather here

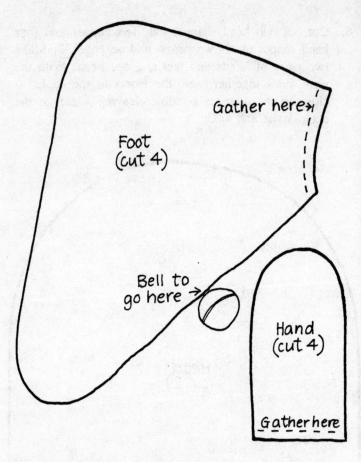

Gather here →

Foot
(cut 4)

Bell to
go here →

Hand
(cut 4)

Gather here

7. Cut two pieces of elastic 30cm long for the legs.

8. Turn the head, hands and feet the right side out and fill them with stuffing.

9. Push the elastic into the gap at the top of the foot. Gather the top edge of the foot using a small running stitch, making sure you catch the elastic at the same time. Work the second foot in the same way.

32

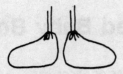

9. With the gathers facing upwards, thread twenty leg circles on to each piece of elastic. Hold the two leg pieces together and thread them on the body circles.

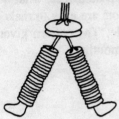

10. Push the ends of the elastic into the neck opening and close the opening as you did for the foot, making sure you sew the elastic very securely.

11. Either sew felt features on to the face or embroider them on. Sew the wool around the head for hair.

12. Sew one hand on to the remaining piece of elastic as you did the feet and face. Thread on eighteen arm circles, right sides facing outwards. Pass the arm elastic between the two pieces of body elastic, three circles below the head. Thread on the remaining arm circles and sew on the other hand.

13. Sew the bells very securely on the clown's feet.

●● Quilted Baby Boots

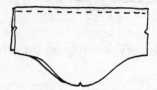

If your baby brother or sister has
got past the knitted bootee stage
but is not yet walking and is
forever suffering from cold feet, what do you do? Here is
an answer. These boots are easy to make, they stay on and
are machine-washable. The pattern given fits a baby aged
from six to twelve months.

You will need

Scissors
20cm of 90cm wide quilted fabric
20cm of 90cm wide lining fabric
31cm of 0.5cm elastic
1m of ribbon *or* piping cord for ties

Instructions

1. Cut out two main shapes in quilted fabric, two main
    shapes in lining fabric, two soles in quilted fabric, and
    two soles in lining fabric.

2. Cut the elastic in half so you have two pieces, each
    15.5cm long. Cut the ribbon so you have two pieces,
    each 50cm long.

3. Work on one boot at a time. With right sides together,
    using a running stitch, join the lining to the quilted
    fabric along the straight edge.

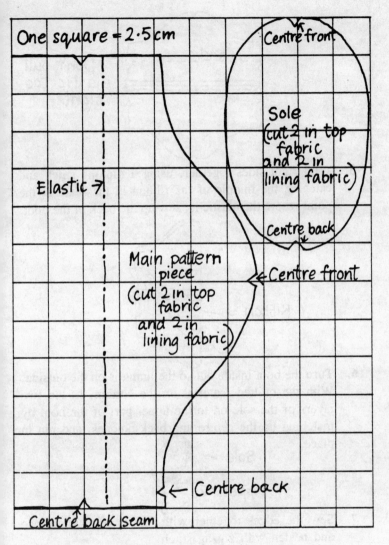

One square = 2.5cm

Centre front

Sole
(cut 2 in top fabric and 2 in lining fabric)

Centre back

← Centre front

Elastic →

Main pattern piece
(cut 2 in top fabric and 2 in lining fabric)

← Centre back

Centre back seam

4. Press the seam open. Using a running stitch, sew the elastic on to the wrong side of the quilted fabric (as marked in pattern). See diagram on page 36.

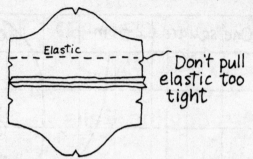

Elastic

Don't pull elastic too tight

5. With right sides together, using a running stitch and catching the middle of the ribbon in the seam at the point where the elastic is, sew up the back of the boot.

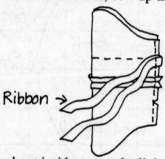

Ribbon →

6. Turn the boot inside out so the lining is on the outside. With the quilted material on the bottom, fit the two layers of the sole on to the upper part of the boot by matching up the centre and back notches, and pin in place.

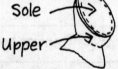

Sole

Upper

7. Sew the edges together with 0.5cm seam allowance and neaten with zigzag stitch.

8. Turn the boot the right side out.

9. Work the second boot in the same way as the first.

Presents for Young Children

● Juggling Balls

These are easy to make and great
fun to play with, and they make a
good present for any age. Make
three per present.

You will need

Pencil
Ruler
Paper
Scissors
Dressmaker's pins
Felt in lots of colours
Needle and thread
Dried beans *or* lentils *or* rice

Instructions

1. Draw six 5cm squares on to a piece of paper.

2. Cut the squares out and pin each one on to a different
   coloured piece of felt.

3. Cut out the felt squares and remove the paper.

4. Sew three of the pieces of felt together, as close to the
   edge as possible. Repeat this process with the other
   3 pieces of felt. See diagram on page 38.

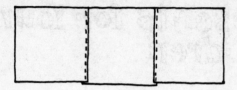

5. Then sew the two three-section pieces together, leaving the last side open, as shown.

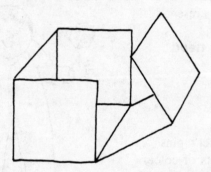

6. Fill the cube with dried beans, peas or lentils. It might be easiest if you use a funnel to help you do this. Close the top of the cube by oversewing.

●● Shoe Bag

You will need

Piece of fabric, 50cm × 76cm
Scissors
Scraps of fabrics for appliqué (optional)
Needle and thread
Safety pin
150cm of piping cord

Instructions

1. Cut the fabric in half so that you have two pieces, each 50cm × 38cm.

2. If you are going to appliqué the bag, (see p. 110) do this on the front of one of the pieces now. If not, go to step 3.

3. With right sides together, sew the fabric pieces together from the top of one side all the way round to within 6cm of the top of the other.

4. Fold over the top 3cm of the material, and sew this flap to the fabric underneath to form a channel for the drawstring, as shown.

5. Thread a safety pin through the end of the piping cord and push this through the channel at the top of the bag.

6. Remove the safety pin and knot the ends of the cord together.

7. Turn the bag the right side out.

●● Bath Mitt

To make bath-time more fun, why
not make an animal bath mitt to be
used instead of a face cloth?

You will need

Pencil and paper
Pins
0.5m of yellow towelling
Thread and needle
Scissors

Instructions

1. Draw round the hand of the person to whom you are
    giving the present.

2. Draw the shape of a duck's foot around the outline of
    the hand as shown. Allow a 1cm seam allowance.

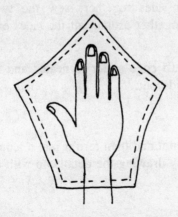

3. Use this drawing as your pattern. Pin it to the towelling and cut out two identical pieces.

4. On one piece of towelling, pin three darts as shown on the pattern, and sew on the right side of the material as close to the edge as possible.

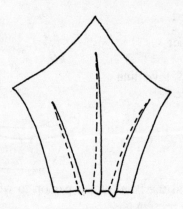

5. With right sides together, sew the two pieces of towelling together around all the sides except for the cuff.

6. Turn the cuff edge under to neaten and turn the mitt the right side out.

Ideas

Make a round mitt and then turn it into a leopard's paw or a fish or frog by drawing the details on with a waterproof felt pen.

 Rag Doll

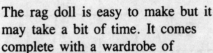 

The rag doll is easy to make but it
may take a bit of time. It comes
complete with a wardrobe of
knickers, petticoat, dress and slippers. By using the basic
pattern but changing the hair length, colour, adding ears or
changing the other features, you can make many different
types of doll.

You will need

Dressmaker's grid paper
Pencil
Scissors
60cm of 90cm calico or natural coloured cotton
20cm of 90cm white or natural knitted cotton (or cut up an
    old vest or T-shirt)
Needle and thread
Kapok for stuffing
Wool
Cardboard
Scraps of white, pink and red felt
Pink fabric paint (optional)
Pink embroidery thread

Instructions

1. Enlarge the patterns on pages 44 and 45 on to grid
    paper.

2. Cut out four arms, four legs and two body sections
    from the calico.

43

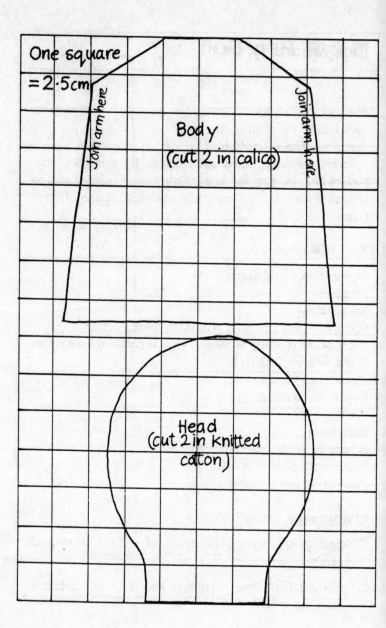

One square
= 2·5cm

Join arm here

Body
(cut 2 in calico)

Join arm here

Head
(cut 2 in knitted
cotton)

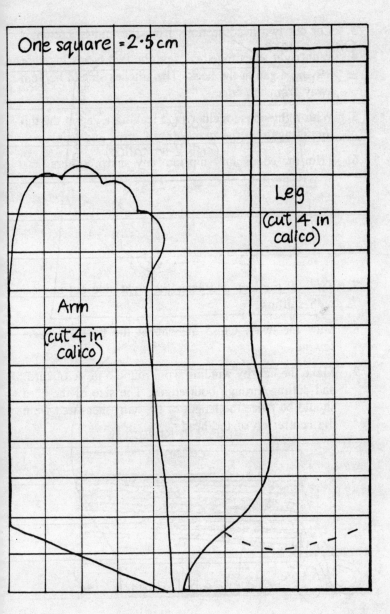

One square = 2·5 cm

Arm
(cut 4 in calico)

Leg
(cut 4 in calico)

45

3. Cut out two head sections from the knitted cotton.

4. With right sides together, sew the two heads together leaving a gap at the neck. The stitches should be 1cm away from the edge.

5. With right sides together, and leaving a gap at the top for filling, sew the two pairs of arms and legs.

6. Trim the edges and snip into any sharp corners.

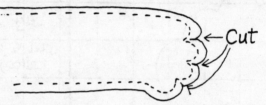

7. Turn all the legs and arms the right side out and fill with stuffing.

8. Stuff the head. Close the gap at the neck by over-sewing.

9. Make the hair by winding wool round a piece of card, and cutting through both edges. The size of the card should be twice the length of the hair, measured from the centre top of the head.

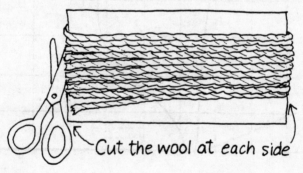

For long hair lay the wool in a strip as below. Sew across the centre of the strip, and sew it on to the head.

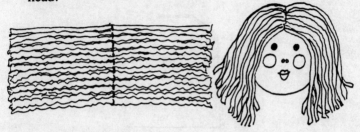

Here are two other styles you might prefer.

10. Paint, sew or embroider the features into place on the face. The cheeks can be painted on in fabric paint. The nose can be made by sewing a circle of running stitches and pulling up into gathers, or by sewing on a small circle of felt. You can also use small circles of felt for the eyes.

11. With right sides out, sandwich an arm between the two body sections and sew into position, catching its raw edges inside the body material.

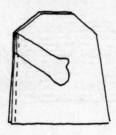

12. Repeat for the other arm.

13. Insert the legs into the body and machine into place.

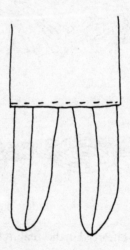

14. Fill the body with stuffing.

15. Place the head into the body, turn in all the raw edges and oversew by hand.

●●● Rag Doll Clothes

You will need

Dressmaker's grid paper
40cm of 90cm fabric for knickers and petticoat
1m of 5cm lace
1m of 1cm lace
Scissors
50cm of 5mm elastic
50cm of small-scale print fabric for dress
20cm of red felt for shoes
Ribbon (optional)
Press studs

Instructions

Knickers

1. Enlarge the pattern on page 50 on to grid paper.

2. Pin the pattern on to the fabric and cut out two knicker shapes.

3. Sew the 5cm lace on to the knicker leg section of each piece, to neaten the edge.

4. With right sides together, sew the knicker front to the back, down the sides and under the crutch.

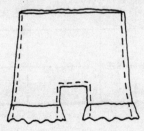

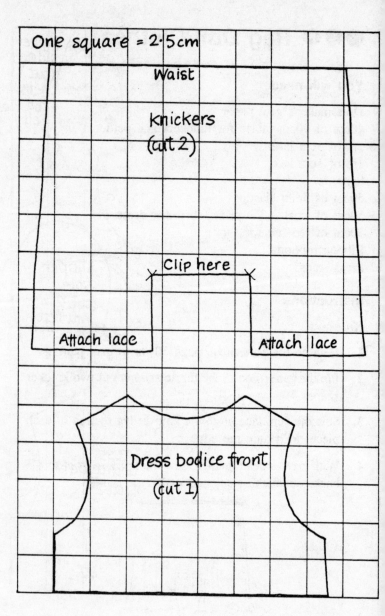

One square = 2·5cm

Waist

Knickers
(cut 2)

Clip here

Attach lace

Attach lace

Dress bodice front
(cut 1)

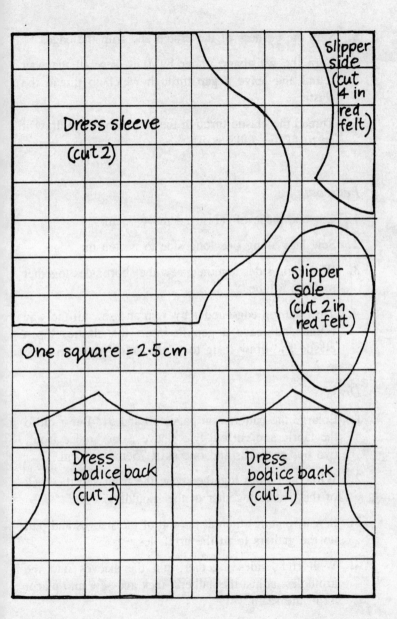

Slipper side
(cut 4 in red felt)

Dress sleeve
(cut 2)

Slipper sole
(cut 2 in red felt)

One square = 2.5 cm

Dress bodice back
(cut 1)

Dress bodice back
(cut 1)

5. Snip the corners of the crutch and trim the edges.

6. Turn the waistband under by 1cm, sew all the way round and leave a gap through which to thread the elastic.

7. Thread the elastic through the waistband, and draw it up to fit the doll's waist.

Petticoat

1. Cut one piece of fabric 20cm × 75cm.

2. Sew lace along one long side to neaten the edge.

3. With right sides together, sew the short sides together to form a tube.

4. Turn the top edge under by 1cm and sew all the way round and leave a gap to insert the elastic. Insert elastic and draw it up to fit the doll's waist.

Dress

1. Enlarge the patterns on pages 50 and 51. Pin it on to the fabric and cut out two sleeves, one bodice front, two bodice backs and one skirt 75cm × 22cm.

2. With right sides together, sew the front and the back of the bodice together at the shoulders.

3. Sew a running stitch at the top of the sleeves and pull up the gathers to fit the armholes.

4. With right sides together, pin the sleeves into the armholes, adjust the gathers, tack and sew into place. Trim the seam.

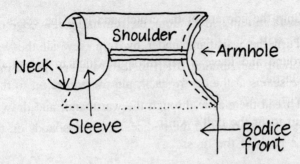

Neck

Shoulder

←Armhole

Sleeve

←—Bodice front

5. Neaten the edge of the seam by sewing on the lace.

6. With right sides together, sew down the side of the sleeve and the bodice seams.

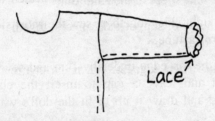

Lace

7. Neaten the back seams by turning them under and under again.

8. Neaten one long edge of the skirt. Sew on the 1cm lace.

9. With right sides together, fold the skirt in half to form a tube. Sew halfway up the short side. Neaten the remainder of the seam you have just sewn.

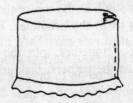

10. Sew a running stitch along the remaining raw edge of the skirt.

11. Pull up the running stitch to form gathers. Matching the seams at the centre back, pin the bodice on to the skirt.

12. Sew the skirt on to the bodice. Sew press studs on to the back of the dress.

13. Tie a large sash round the doll's waist.

Slippers

Work first one slipper, then the other.

1. Sew the two slipper-side pieces together down the centre back seam.

2. Sew the fronts together down the centre front seam.

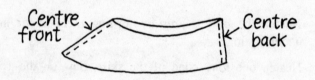

3. With right sides together, pin, then sew the tops on to the soles.

4. Turn the slipper the right side out and put it on the doll's foot. Adjustments may have to be made at this stage, depending on how much stuffing is in each foot. You can tack the shoe on to the foot to stop it coming off. Sew tiny bows on to the centre front to decorate.

●●● Dressing Up Clothes

From our super all-in-one pattern you can make a variety of exciting costumes for children aged from four to six. Simply lengthen or shorten the arms and legs as necessary.

Spaceman

To make the spaceman's suit use grey polyester cotton with silver lamé for the details. (If you don't mind the costume feeling stiff, you could use silver spray paint instead.) The accessories are an old crash helmet and a pair of wellington boots, both sprayed silver. A belt with a silver buckle completes the outfit.

Clown

Make a clown suit from bits and pieces of brightly coloured remnants, with lots of ribbons as accessories. Use face paint for the clown's face, and an old ping pong ball with a cross cut into the back of it so it will fit over the nose. Paint the nose with red paint. Wear a pair of large flippers on your feet.

Animal

Depending on the kind of fur available, our basic pattern can turn you into a cat, rabbit, bear, mouse or tiger. The accessories consist of different kinds of ears and tails. The same instructions apply for all three costumes.

You will need

For all costumes:
Dressmaker's grid paper
Pencil
Scissors
40cm zipper *or* the same amount of velcro, *or* poppers on a strip
Needle and thread
Pins

For animal costume:
3m of fur fabric
50cm of lining fabric
40cm of felt for earlining
Press studs for neck
Kapok, wadding or old tights for stuffing the tail

For clown suit:
2.1m of fabric
1m of elastic for cuffs and bottom of legs
Lots of brightly coloured contrasting ribbon

For spaceman:
2.1m of fabric
50cm of silver or gold lamé fabric.

Instructions

1. Enlarge the patterns on pages 61 and 62 on to dressmaker's grid paper. Cut out your pattern pieces.

2. Fold the material in half and place the pattern pieces on one side. Cut through the double layer of material to make two fronts, two backs, and two arms for each costume. (Remember that if you are using a 'pile' fabric for the animal costume, make sure the pile goes

56

in the same direction on each pattern piece.) If you are
making an animal, cut out ears, hood (and their
linings) and tail, in addition to the other pattern pieces.
If you are making the spaceman suit, cut a front and
back panel and two cuffs and a collar from lamé.

3. With right sides together, sew the two fronts together
   as marked on the diagram.

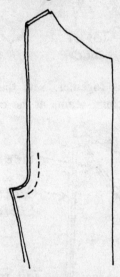

4. Sew in the zipper or poppers or velcro on the rest of
   the centre front.

5. With right sides together, sew the two backs together
   down the centre back seam. If you are making an
   animal, leave a gap for the tail as marked on the
   pattern.

6. Sew the darts on the shoulder seams.

7. With the right sides together, pin the sleeves to the

edges of the armholes, front and back, and sew them into position.

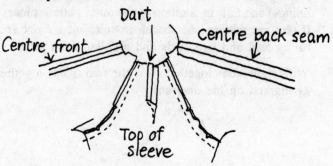

8. With right sides together, sew the underarms, and inside leg, matching seams at the centre.

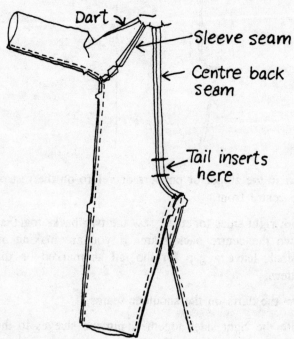

9. To neaten all the seams, turn them under by 5mm an again by 5mm, and sew with a running stitch.

For Clown

Sew ribbon around the sleeves and trouser legs, about 5cm from the edge. Thread with elastic.

Add patch pockets and other decorative ribbons. A ribbon gathered along one edge makes a pretty collar.

For Spaceman

Appliqué the front and back panels in place, as shown in the diagram.

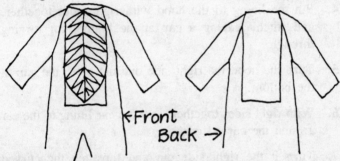

←Front

Back →

Make epaulettes from lamé filled with wadding, and topstitched. Attach them at the shoulders.

Attach collar and cuffs as shown in the diagram.

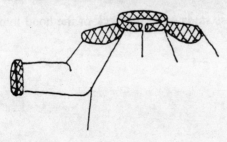

For Animal

Make a tail by sewing the two pieces together with right sides facing. Stuff the tail, turn it the right side out and insert it in the gap. For a rabbit, make a white wool pompom tail (see page 70 for Baby's Pompom Ball).

Make a hood:

1. Sew darts.

2. With right sides together, sew the two pieces together along the centre back seam.

3. Make the hood lining in the same way.

4. Pin the lining to the hood with right sides together, and stitch, leaving a gap at the bottom for turning through.

5. Turn the hood the right side out and close the gap at the bottom.

6. With right sides together, sew the ear lining to the ear around the curved edges.

7. Turn it the right side out and topstitch the curved edges.

8. Make a pleat as indicated on the pattern and pin on the hood. When you feel they look OK, sew into place.

9. Sew press studs on to the neck of the hood to close it.

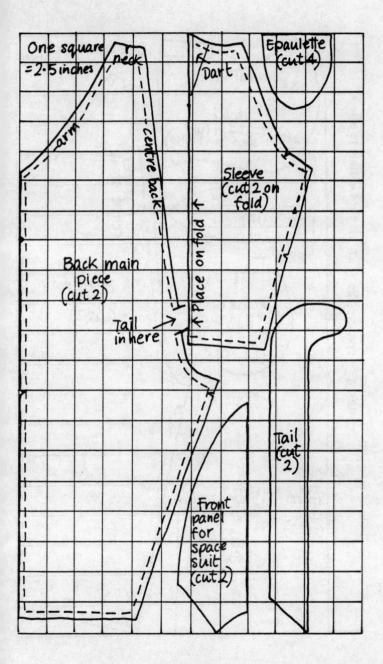

One square = 2.5 inches

neck

arm

centre back

Dart

Epaulette (cut 4)

Sleeve (cut 2 on fold)

Place on fold

Back main piece (cut 2)

Tail in here

Tail (cut 2)

Front panel for space suit (cut 2)

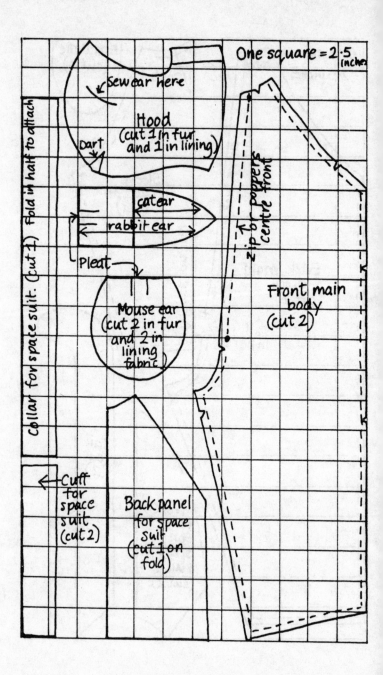

One square = 2.5 inches

Sew ear here

Hood
(cut 1 in fur
and 1 in lining)

Dart

Collar for space suit. (cut 1) Fold in half to attach

cat ear

rabbit ear

Pleat

Mouse ear
(cut 2 in fur
and 2 in
lining
fabric)

zip or poppers
centre front

Front main
body
(cut 2)

Cuff
for
space
suit
(cut 2)

Back panel
for space
suit
(cut 1 on
fold)

●●● Dream Castle

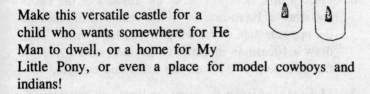

Make this versatile castle for a
child who wants somewhere for He
Man to dwell, or a home for My
Little Pony, or even a place for model cowboys and
indians!

You will need

Scissors
Cardboard box big enough for the toy figures to go in
Sharp craft knife or bread knife (with your parents'
    permission)
Four cardboard tubes (you can often get these at drawing
    offices, fabric shops or photocopying shops)
Pencil
Ruler
Brown sticky tape
Non-toxic paint
Small piece of fabric for flag
Fabric felt tips to decorate

Instructions

1. Cut the top off the cardboard box and keep the pieces.

2. Using the craft knife or bread knife, cut the tubes so
    that they are the same size as each other but taller than
    the box.

3. Draw the windows and mark the turrets on the top of
    each tube. Cut these out using a craft knife.

4. Mark and cut out the turrets on the top of the box.

5. Draw and cut out the doorway in one long side of the box.

6. Place a tube next to one of the corners of the castle and draw a 10cm-line down the centre of the tube on the opposite side to the window you have made. Then draw a 10cm-line in the same position on a corner of the box. Repeat with all the tubes and corners.

7. Make slits at intervals along the lines you have drawn.

8. Using the pieces of card saved from the top of the box, wedge them into the slits on the tubes and into the corners of the box.

9. Tape the card into position on the inside of the box.

10. Avoiding the windows, wrap brown sticky tape round the tubes on the outside of the box to stabilize the whole building.

11. Use any leftover card to make the castle battlements. Cut pieces of card the length of each side of the box and as wide as needed for the toy figures to stand on.

12. Tape the card into position making sure that the toy figures can see over the top of the castle walls.

13. Paint the castle.

14. Make the flag by decorating a small piece of fabric with felt tips. Stick it on a lolly stick or knitting needle and tape this to the inside of one of the tubes.

Next to Nothing Presents

Just because you are broke and without funds does not mean that you must be excluded from giving presents. These presents cost very little to make. All you need are a little time and ingenuity.

●● Baby Bear

You will need

An old woollen or knitted glove
Scissors
Needle and thread
Old tights for stuffing (wash them first)
Piece of wool
Scraps of felt or other fabric
Fabric glue
Embroidery thread *or* fabric felt tips
Piece of ribbon

Instructions

1. Turn the glove inside out.

2. Cut off the middle finger and put it to one side.

3. Oversew the hole made by the absent finger, to close it.

4. Turn the glove round so the fingers are pointing downwards.

5. Fill all the fingers and the main part of the glove with stuffing.

6. Sew up the wrist opening.

7. Tie a piece of wool just above the fingers to make the head.

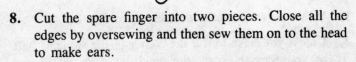

8. Cut the spare finger into two pieces. Close all the edges by oversewing and then sew them on to the head to make ears.

9. Cut out eyes and a nose from scraps of felt and stick or sew them into place. Embroider or draw a mouth on the face.

10. Finish off by tying a ribbon round the neck.

● Pebble Paper Weight

When you next go to the seaside,
collect shells for making pretty
picture frames and large pebbles or
stones for paper weights. Let the shape and colour of the
stone suggest to you the image you will paint.

You will need

Large smooth flat stone
White or light emulsion paint
Paintbrushes
Pencil
Water colour or poster paint
Clear varnish (nail varnish will do)

Instructions

1. Wash the stone and then leave it to dry.

2. Unless you wish to use the colour of the stone as part
   of your design, paint the emulsion paint on to one
   side. Leave it to dry.

3. Paint the other side of the stone and leave it to dry.

4. Using the pencil, draw a design on the stone. You
   might want to draw an animal, landscape, abstract
   pattern, fish or birds, for example.

5. Mix your water colours or poster paints fairly thickly
   so that the colour is intense, and then paint on your
   design.

6. When the paint is dry, give the stone a coat of clear
   varnish.

●●● Patchwork Oven Cloth

Use up bits of old material to make
a pretty, decorative oven cloth.

You will need

Scraps of cotton fabric for the patchwork
Terry towelling for the lining
Wadding for the filling
Pins
Needle and thread
Contrast bias binding
(Brass curtain rings optional)

Instructions

1. Make a small shape out of patchwork (see *Crazy Sewing* for patchwork).

2. Cut out the lining and the wadding, using your patchwork shape as a guide.

3. Pin the wadding to the back of the patchwork, and then pin the towelling underneath.

4. Sew the layers together as close to the edge as possible.

5. Neaten the edges by covering them with bias binding.

6. Sew the brass ring on to the corner so that you can hang up the oven cloth. Or make a loop from bias binding.

69

●● Baby's Pompom Ball

Pompoms can be made from scraps
of knitting yarn, or even unpicked
sweaters if you don't mind your
pompoms being crinkly. Make a large one to hang from a
baby's pram or crib, use them to decorate socks or
sweaters, or make them into animals.

You will need

Pencil
Plate
2 pieces of cardboard, approximately 20cm square
225g (8oz) knitting yarn (wool or acrylic or nylon)
Ruler
Scissors
Lid of a coffee jar
Shirring elastic

Instructions

1. Draw round the plate on both pieces of card.

2. Cut out the circles.

3. Place the coffee jar lid in the centre of one circle and
   draw round it, then do the same with the other circle.
   Cut out the centres, so that you are left with two halo
   shapes.

4. Put one piece of card on top of the other.

5. Wind the wool round and round the cards until all the
   card is covered and the hole in the middle is quite
   small.

6. Carefully cut around the edge of the wool circle keeping one of the scissor blades between the pieces of card.

7. Pull the circles apart slightly. Tie a piece of wool very tightly around the centre of the ball.

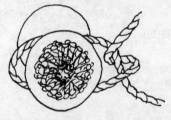

8. Remove the card and fluff out the ball.

9. Tie a piece of shirring elastic from the centre and hang the pompom up.

Ideas

To make a spider, make one large pompom and one small one in black, and add red pipe-cleaner legs.

●● Papier Mâché Vase

Papier Mâché is very easy to make and you can achieve very sophisticated results for very little money.

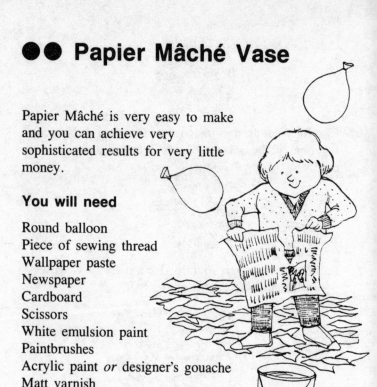

You will need

Round balloon
Piece of sewing thread
Wallpaper paste
Newspaper
Cardboard
Scissors
White emulsion paint
Paintbrushes
Acrylic paint *or* designer's gouache
Matt varnish

Before you start

Although the papier mâché process is very simple, it does take time as each layer has to dry before the next can be added. The drying time may vary from that given, depending on the temperature in which you work. Allow about twelve days to complete a large vase.

You need a kitchen table on which to work, and somewhere to hang the balloon while it dries.

Instructions

1. Blow up the balloon and tie a knot in it.

2. Tie a piece of thread around the knot.

3. Following the maker's instructions, mix the wallpaper paste with water until it is the consistency of double cream.

4. Rip up the newspaper into pieces approximately 10cm square.

5. Dip a piece of paper into the glue, and stick it on to the balloon, smoothing it into position. Repeat this process with the next piece of paper, overlapping the first piece as you stick it into position.

6. Continue papering the balloon, overlapping each piece of paper until the balloon is completely covered. Make sure that each piece of paper is smoothed into position. Leave the thread free and hang the balloon in a doorway to dry overnight.

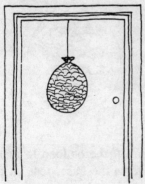

7. On the following day, cover the balloon in another layer of paper and leave this to dry. Altogether you will need to cover the balloon eight times, allowing each layer to dry before applying the next.

8. When the eight layers of paper are dry, pop the balloon and either tear or cut a hole at the top of the papier mâché shape for the vase opening. Pull out the balloon.

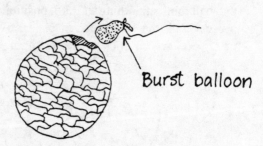

Burst balloon

9. You may wish to make a lip or funnel neck for the vase. Shape this with more papier mâché. You can staple, tape or glue a neck made from cardboard into place and then papier mâché over this.

10. Cut the bottom off the balloon to make a flat base to the vase. To form the base, tear strips of newspaper long enough to cover the gap. Dip these strips in glue and smooth them across the opening, overlapping each piece.

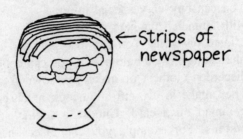

←Strips of newspaper

11. The neck and the base will need about three layers of papier mâché and will have to dry between each layer.

12. Paint the inside and outside of the vase with white emulsion paint.

13. Decorate the vase using acrylic paint or designer's gouache.

14. To complete the vase, paint it with a coat of matt varnish.

● Buttons on a Card

You can buy very special buttons
with animals, numbers or flowers
printed on them. You can also get
interesting shaped buttons. Or you can collect buttons from
discarded clothes, or make your own from Fimo (p. 96)
They make lovely gifts, but look much better if they are
mounted on a card. Choose a setting suitable for your
buttons. For example you can place sheep buttons in a
landscape, duck buttons on a pond, and bows on a dress.

You will need

Pencil
Plain white card (plain postcards are good)
Felt tips
Scissors
Needle and thread
Scissors
Buttons

Instructions

1. Draw a scene or decorative border on your card.
   Colour it in.

2. Mark where you wish to place the buttons with a
   pencil.

3. Thread the needle and tie a knot in the end. Sew the
   buttons in place on the card. Make sure you knot the
   buttons securely on the back of the card.

● Haberdashery Drawers

For people interested in sewing, and even those who only sew buttons on but can never find a pin, needle or shirt button, this tidy has to be the answer.

Collect hooks, eyes and other bits and pieces to put in the drawers from old clothes. Buy some needles and pins.

You will need

Six large matchboxes
Glue
Ruler
Wrapping paper
Pencil
Scissors
Six square wooden beads
Assorted haberdashery

Instructions

1. Stick the matchboxes together as shown so that all the drawers face to the front.

2. Measure the matchbox from front to back.

3. Cut a piece of wrapping paper the same length as the matchbox, and wrap it round the drawers.

Wrapping paper

Length of matchbox

4. Mark with a pencil where the two edges overlap by 2cm.

5. Cut where you have marked.

6. Stick the wrapping paper on the drawers.

7. Stick the beads on to the drawers to use as handles.

8. Fill the drawers with haberdashery.

● New from Old

Before throwing anything away, see if it can be recycled.

Keep a box or tin for old buttons.

Always cut zips off old clothes as these are expensive to buy.

An odd sock or glove can be turned into a puppet.

An old pompom hat can be turned into a tea cosy by cutting holes for the handle and spout and binding the edges to stop them fraying.

Keep old tights for stuffing soft toys or cushions.

Turn an old pair of jeans into a bag by turning them inside out, cutting off the legs and sewing across the bottom with a back stitch. Then turn right side out and sew a strap from one side to the other to make a shoulder bag.

Keep bits of leftover wool and use them for french knitting, crocheting, or knitting.

Boxes and tins can be redecorated and used as gift boxes.

Large pieces of material, such as curtains, sheets, blankets or old tablecloths, can be used for numerous projects. Here are just a few:

1. Turn an old blanket into a poncho. This is a kind of cloak but instead of opening at the front, it has a hole in the middle that goes over the head. If the blanket is rather dull, decorate it with embroidery or beads, or cover it with old buttons.

2. An old velvet curtain will make a luxurious cloak. If your curtain is faded or has holes in places, then decorate it with appliqué.

3. Old sheets can be tied to a clothes horse or thrown over a washing line or table to make a tent or house.

● IOU Presents

If you are very broke, perhaps you have a skill you could give as a present. Since you can't really wrap this up in gift paper, you can always write the present on a card, for example 'IOU three weeks' worth of ironing'! Below are a few ideas to set you thinking.

Baby Sitting

You may get on very well with young children. How about offering to baby-sit as a present for a harassed aunt or mother who would love to have some time to herself?

Reading

You may be good at reading, in which case you could offer to read the bedtime story to younger brothers and sisters.

Or you could help a young one who is struggling with learning to read.

Or you could read to an elderly relative or friend whose sight is going, but would like to know what is in the newspapers.

A Diet Aid

Is one of your parents fighting the battle of the bulge? How about you helping? Stick pictures of fatties and the word NO in big letters on the fridge door and the biscuit tin. Cut up slivers of carrots and celery and leave them ready in the fridge for the moment the bulging parent is tempted!

Car Cleaning and Other Chores

No one likes a dirty car, so why don't you offer a valet service, and clean the inside and outside of the car? Don't forget to empty the ash trays, and wipe the sticky seats.

If you are good at ironing you can offer to do the ironing for the next three weeks.

If you enjoy gardening, you could do the weeding one weekend.

Or you can feed the pets and clean out their cages for a few weeks.

Presents for the Very Old

All children think their parents and grandparents are old. But this section is not for those of you with windsurfing grannies — it is for the very old who may not be able to get about as much as they used to.

●● Foot Warmer

As you get older it is often your extremities — your hands and feet — that suffer from the cold. So a foot warmer in which you can put your feet in while you snuggle up in front of the television is a good idea.

You will need

A light-coloured pillow case
Dressmaker's pins
Piece of card
Fabric pens
Iron and ironing board
Enough polyester wadding to fit round the pillow case (approximately 0.5m)
Needle and thread

Instructions

1. Fold the pillow case in half and mark the fold-line

with a row of pins on the front and back.

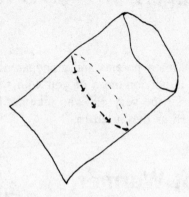

2. Put a piece of card inside the pillow case and draw on your design on the fabric, up to the pin line, in fabric pens.

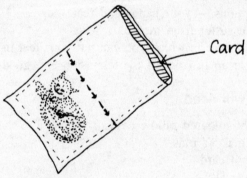

Card

3. Turn the pillow case over and draw a design on the back, up to the line of pins.

4. Turn the pillow case inside out and iron it to fix the design.

5. Cut a piece of wadding the same length as the pillow case but twice as wide.

6. Wrap the wadding round the pillow case and sew it into place at the side seams and at the top edge.

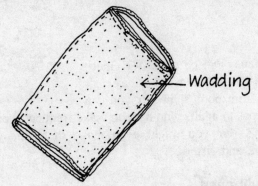

Wadding

7. Turn the pillow case the right side out, and then fold the top part in at the line of pins so that the wadding is sandwiched in the pillow case.

8. Turn the footwarmer inside out and pin the bottom edges. Oversew to hide the wadding. Remove all the pins and turn the right side out before giving the present away.

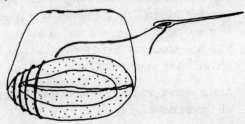

85

● Story Tape

Story tapes can be made for elderly
friends and relations who may
suffer from poor sight. Or you can
give tapes to adults who have to make frequent, boring car
journeys. Or you might even make them for younger
brothers and sisters.

You will need

Book from which to read
Access to a cassette recorder
Cassette tape
Lots of time and a quiet room in which to read

Instructions

1. Read the book, or at least the first chapter, before you
   begin to record. Check any words that you don't know
   the meaning of in the dictionary.

2. Practise reading the chapter aloud. Remember to
   speak clearly but naturally. Do not go too fast.

3. Have a practice recording, then play it back to
   yourself to see how it sounds. If it is good, carry on.
   If it sounds strange, try and work out why. Perhaps
   you are speaking too slowly, or too quickly. Then
   record over your mistakes.

4. Make your own cassette label and stick it on the cover
   of the cassette.

●● Perfumed Flowers

One usually thinks of flowers being
beautiful to look at, which they
are. However, they can also be
very beautiful to smell. People who have lost one of their
senses often have their others heightened by that loss, so
that a blind person may hear better or have a greater sense
of smell, than a sighted person.

Hyacinths are one of the most perfumed flowers that you
can find. Allow about three months for them to grow!

You will need

Gravel or pieces of broken pot
Flower pot
Saucer
Compost
Hyacinth bulbs
Water

Instructions

1. Put some pieces of broken pot or gravel in the bottom
   of the flower pot. Place the pot on a saucer.

2. Half-fill the pot with compost.

3. Put the bulbs close together on top of the compost,
   with the pointed ends facing upwards, and then fill the
   pot with more compost. The top of the bulbs should
   just poke out of the compost.

87

4. Water the compost so it is damp, not soaking wet.

5. Put the pot of bulbs in a cool damp place for eight to ten weeks, when the bulbs will begin to bud. Check regularly that the compost is damp, and water it if it is drying up.

6. When the buds are about 5cm high, move the pot to a light, cool place. Remember to water them regularly.

7. As the flowers begin to open, then the plants can be moved to a warmer place and you can put sticks in the compost to prevent the plants from falling over.

● Pomanders

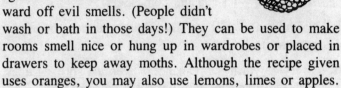

Pomanders were used in the middle
ages and in Elizabethan times to
ward off evil smells. (People didn't
wash or bath in those days!) They can be used to make
rooms smell nice or hung up in wardrobes or placed in
drawers to keep away moths. Although the recipe given
uses oranges, you may also use lemons, limes or apples.

You will need

Small mixing bowl
160g (4 oz) cinnamon powder
50g (2 oz) powdered cloves
12.5g (½ oz) powdered allspice
12.5g (½ oz) powdered nutmeg
25g (1 oz) powdered orris root (obtainable from chemists)
Thin knitting needle
Firm, blemish free, thin-skinned oranges
Whole large-headed cloves
Large ceramic mixing bowl

Make the pomanders one month before giving them away.

Instructions

1. Blend the powders together in the small mixing bowl.
    This is the fixing mixture. (Note: when you have
    finished with it, this mixture can be stored in a plastic
    bag and used over and over again.)

2. Using the needle, make a hole in the skin of an orange
    and then stick a clove in the hole.

3. Repeat step 2, until all of the orange is covered in cloves. If you wish to hang your pomander from a ribbon, leave a path around the orange the width of your ribbon.

4. Sprinkle half the fixing mixture in the bottom of the large bowl, and add the pomanders.

5. Sprinkle the rest of the fixing mixture over the pomanders.

6. Every day turn the pomanders over and sprinkle them with the fixing mixture until they become hard. This may take from two weeks to a month. Once they are hard they are ready to use.

● Pot Pourri

A pot pourri is a mixture of flower petals and spices presented in a pretty bowl and kept in a room to make it smell nice.

You will need

Rose petals
Other flowers, such as carnations, honeysuckle, lavender, orange blossom, pinks
Grater
Small lemon
Small orange
Orris root (obtainable from chemists)
1 tablespoon of mixed spice
Concentrated lavender or rose oil (available from chemists)
Airtight jar with screw lid

Make the pot pourri two months before giving it away.

Instructions

1. Pick the flowers before they are fully opened.

2. Pull off the petals and spread them out to dry on a piece of paper, away from sunlight.

3. Turn them twice a day until they are as dry as corn-flakes. They can take up to two weeks to dry.

4. Grate the peel from the lemon and orange into a mixing bowl and add the dried flowers.

5. Add the orris root and mixed spice.

6. Add a few drops of the flower oil.

7. Store the mixture in an airtight jar for six weeks to dry in a warm place. Shake the jar each day.

8. After six weeks transfer the pot pourri to a pretty bowl.

●● Tea Cosy

You will need

Grid paper
Pencil
Scissors
35cm of 90cm striped fabric (for lining)
35cm of 90cm black fabric (for outer part of cosy)
Wadding
Remnants of different patterned fabrics in black and white
Needle and black or white sewing thread
Black and white ribbons

Instructions

1. Enlarge the pattern shown on p. 94.

2. Cut out two tea cosy shapes in striped fabric, two in black fabric, and two in wadding.

3. Cut out wedges, as shown in the pattern, from the fabric remnants, and pin them on to one of the black fabric pieces.

4. Tack and then sew these wedges into position.

5. Sew on ribbons to cover the joins.

Ribbon

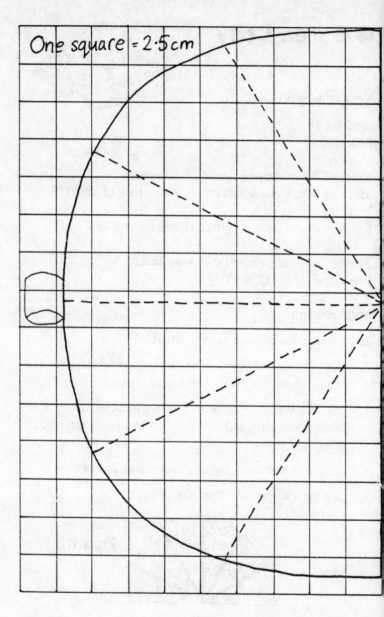

One square = 2.5cm

6. With right sides together, sew the back of the tea cosy to the front around the curved edge. Press.

7. With the right sides together, sew the front and back lining pieces together around the curved edge. Turn it the right side out and press.

8. Sandwich the lining between the two layers of wadding and sew around the curved edge.

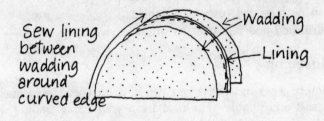

Sew lining between wadding around curved edge

Wadding

Lining

9. Fit the lining and the wadding into the outer part of the cosy and neaten it with a hem stitch.

10. Make a bow to sew on to the top point of the wedges.

11. Make a ribbon loop from which to hang the cosy.

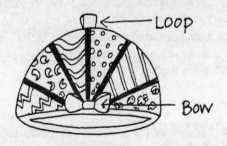

Loop

Bow

Decorative Presents

●●● Fimo Buttons

Fimo is a modelling material that
comes in a variety of colours and
can be moulded, carved, marbled,
varnished and baked in an ordinary oven.

Kneading

Before working with Fimo you have to knead it to make
it soft and pliable. The heat from your hands should do
this. Just put a ball of Fimo in your hands and squeeze it.

Rolling out

You can roll out Fimo with a rolling pin in the same way
that you roll out pastry.

Modelling

You can cut and shape pieces of Fimo to form such things
as leaves and flowers. So instead of making round buttons,
why not make all different shapes, including geometric
ones, such as elongated triangles, squares, rectangles,
stars and diamonds.

Marbling

You can mix two or more colours of Fimo and knead them
together to obtain a marbled effect.

Hardening

(An oven is used to harden the Fimo so be careful and make sure an adult is around and that you have permission to use the oven.)

Pre-heat the oven to 140°C/275°F/Gas mark 1. Place aluminium foil on a baking tray and put the shaped Fimo to be baked on the foil. Bake for between fifteen to twenty minutes, depending on the size of the object to be baked. Check that the object does not overcook or else it will go brown.

Varnishing

You can buy special lacquer for Fimo or you can use clear nail varnish to give a protective coat.

Mould making

You can also use Fimo to make a mould. This is particularly good when you want to make buttons all the same size. If you have something with a raised surface that you wish to copy, roll out a piece of Fimo. Press the object into the Fimo and then lift it out, leaving an impression. Coins are very good for making impressions. The Fimo with the impression should then be baked to make a mould.

To make lots of copies of your original, simply press Fimo into the mould and then lift out the shape. You may need to trim the shapes when they are lifted out. Remember to make the holes in the button before baking. Do this with a skewer. Then bake the button shapes in the oven.

●●● Christmas Stocking Buttons

You will need

Tracing paper
Pencil and scissors
Rolling pin
Fimo in red, green and white (or other colours if you
    prefer)
Small kitchen knife *or* craft knife
Embroidery needle
Baking tray
Clear nail varnish

Instructions

1. Trace the design below on to tracing paper.

2. Cut out the design and use it as a template.

3. Roll out the green Fimo and place the template on top
   of the Fimo.

4. Cut out as many boot-shaped buttons as required using
   a kitchen knife or craft knife.

5. Decorate the buttons with balls, zigzags and blobs of different coloured Fimo.

6. Make two button holes in each button with the needle.

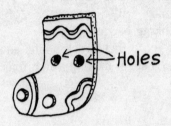

7. Lay the buttons on a baking tray and bake in the oven for approximately fifteen minutes.

8. Leave the baked buttons to cool and then varnish them.

9. Sew the buttons on to button card before giving them as a present.

●●● Cut Ply Badges

If you can master sawing plywood
then you can make very
professional looking badges. If you
find the sawing too difficult, ask a kind adult to help with
this bit of the badge making, and finish the rest by
yourself.

You will need

3mm or 3.5mm plywood (sometimes known as 3ply)
Pencil
Coarse and fine sandpaper
Acrylic or poster paints for decorating
Non-toxic varnish (polyurethane is ideal but you can use
   clear nail varnish)
A brooch back (available from any good haberdashers)
Wood glue or other strong glue

Equipment

Kitchen table or workbench to work on
Jeweller's peg and clamp
Hand fretsaw and lots of blades

Instructions

1. Before starting to saw, practise on a spare piece of
    plywood. Hold the piece of wood you are working on
    over the V shape in the jeweller's peg. Fit a blade into
    the saw with the teeth facing away from the handle.

Saw through the wood with an up and down action at 90 degrees to the wood.

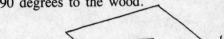

Jeweller's peg

2. Using a pencil, draw the design on the plywood. Keep the shape fairly simple until you get good at sawing. Letters are a good idea or a simple shape like those illustrated.

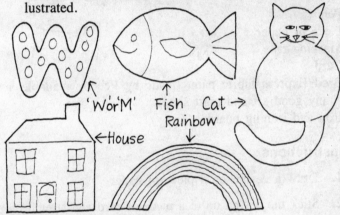

'WorM'
Fish   Cat →
Rainbow
←House

3. Saw round the shape you have drawn.

4. Then, using coarse sandpaper, sand round all the edges until they are smooth.

5. Then sand around all the edges with fine sandpaper.

6. Paint on your design.

7. When the paint is dry, apply varnish.

8. Leave the varnish to dry and then stick on the brooch back.

●● Puffed T-shirt

These T-shirts are decorated with a paint that expands upon heating, so that the design is raised above the surface which it decorates.

You will need

Pen
Piece of paper
Masking tape
Card
Brod Express fabric paint (made by Pebco, available at any good art and craft shop)
Iron and ironing board

Instructions

1. Draw a design on a piece of paper.

2. Stick the design on to a piece of card and stretch the T-shirt over the card. Fasten it down with masking tape.

3. Using the puffy paint, Brod Express, follow the design and paint on the T-shirt.

4. Leave the paint to dry for twenty to thirty minutes before fixing. This can be done by ironing on the back of the design for fifteen seconds, with the iron set on a silk or wool setting.

●●● Silk Painting

Silk is a lovely gift, and a piece of hand-painted silk is the ultimate in luxury. However, the materials are not cheap so read the instructions carefully and do all the preparation required.

The silk painting in this book is done using a gutta outline. This is a gum-like solution which acts as a barrier, separating the colours from one another. It looks a little like the lead in a stained glass window. The colour is applied with a clean paintbrush and it spreads up to the line of gutta. All the materials used are available from good craft or haberdasher shops.

You will need

Paper
Pencil
Silk
Black felt tip
Silk pins for stretching (you can use drawing pins but they
    tend to make holes in the silk)
A frame, on which to pin the silk
Masking tape
Gutta
Applicator
Gutta solvent
Paintbrush
Silk paints and fixative

Instructions

1. Draw your design in pencil on the paper. Make sure the design will fit on your piece of silk, with enough border left for rolling the edge if it is to be a scarf.

2. Go over the design with a black felt tip.

3. Using the silk pins, begin to stretch your silk across the frame, starting in the middle of one side and pinning it down first to the left and then to the right. Do the opposite side in the same way and then the other two sides.

4. Tape your design to the underside of the silk, sticking the tape to the sides of the frame.

5. Then paint on the gutta through the applicator (a bottle with a plastic ball at the end). Using a pin, pierce a hole in the ball of the applicator from the inside, then fill the applicator with gutta. When using the applicator turn it upside down regularly to prevent air locks and bubbles. Add gutta solvent if the gutta becomes too thick. Follow the lines of your design. Make sure all the lines of gutta are joined up, as any gaps will allow the silk paint to trickle through.

6. Before painting the silk, hold the piece up to the light and check that the gutta has penetrated the silk. If not, apply some more. Leave the gutta to dry for one hour before painting.

7. Use a soft brush to apply the paint. Place the loaded brush between the lines of gutta and let the colour creep up to the lines. Rinse the brush in water before using the next colour.

8. Once the design is finished and dry, follow the paint

manufacturer's instructions for fixing.

9. If you are making a scarf, roll the edges of the material to stop it from fraying. Or frame it if it is to be a picture. You can even make a tie or an evening purse from it.

● Decorated Leather Tie

This is a fun present for the man
in your life.

You will need

Plain leather tie in a light colour
Leather dyes
Artist's paintbrush

Instructions

1. Either paint a design directly on to the tie or draw it
    on a piece of paper first and then copy it on to the tie.
    If you are not very good at drawing, do a flicked
    design like a Jackson Pollock painting. Or you could
    draw a keyboard or a treble clef for the musician in
    your family.

2. Leave the dye to dry before wrapping up the present.

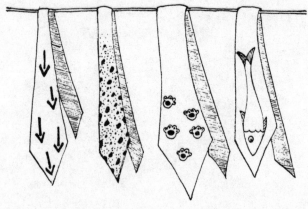

●● Book plates and Preserve labels

Book plates are pretty labels which you stick in the front of a book to say who owns it. Preserve labels are stuck on to jam jars stating the contents and date of use or date made.

You will need

Pencil
Ruler
Felt tip pens
Sticky back labels

Instructions

1. Draw a pretty border or design on your labels, leaving room for the person's name.

2. If it is a book plate, write or stencil THIS BOOK BELONGS TO on the label. Then leave a blank space for the person's name.

You can also use these labels on jars of dried herbs or pot pourri.

●● Birthday Cake Tin

Decorative tins are great fun but
can be expensive to buy, so why
not make your own? You can
decorate a plain round cake tin to look like a birthday or
Christmas cake.

You will need

Pencil
Paper
Felt tips
Cake tin
Indelible felt tip
Ceramic paints
Turpentine substitute
Fine artist's brush
Ceramic varnish

Instructions

1. Draw your design on to paper, and colour it in using
    felt tips.

2. Copy it on to the tin using an indelible felt tip.

3. Follow the line with a black ceramic line. Wash out
    your brush in turpentine substitute.

4. Colour in the main features of your design using very
    bright ceramic colours — cherry red, lavender blue,
    orange yellow and victoria green.

5. Fill in the background patterns with contrasting

colours. Wash the brush in turpentine substitute.

6. Leave the tin to dry for at least forty-eight hours.

7. When the paint is dry, finish off with a protective coat of ceramic varnish.

Idea

Bake a cake to go in the tin for an extra surprise gift!

●●● Appliquéd Evening Bags

These sparkling satin evening bags
are much easier to make than they
look. The decoration is not painted,
embroidered or sewn, but stuck on with a glue-
impregnated sheet called Bondaweb. Bondaweb is made by
Vilene and available in most good haberdashery depart-
ments. As different fabrics may need to be ironed on at
different temperatures, it is best to follow the maker's instructions.

Although I would not recommend Bondaweb for large
areas of fabric which are to get a lot of use, it is ideal for
this purpose, as the areas are small and an evening bag will
not be used every evening.

You will need

Grid paper
Scissors
30cm white slipper satin for a round bag
30cm black slipper satin for decorating the round bag
50cm slipper satin in main colour for an oval bag with bias
    trim
Oddments of other colours for decorating the oval bag
30cm thin polyester wadding for each bag
2m of black cord for the round white bag
Bondaweb
Iron and ironing board
Press stud
Braid for trimming

Instructions

For an oval bag

1. Enlarge the patterns for the bag on pages 112 and 113.

2. Cut out two pieces of each shape in satin and one in wadding.

3. Iron the fabric to be appliquéd on to the Bondaweb following the maker's instructions.

4. Cut out the motifs following the patterns below or you can create some designs of your own.

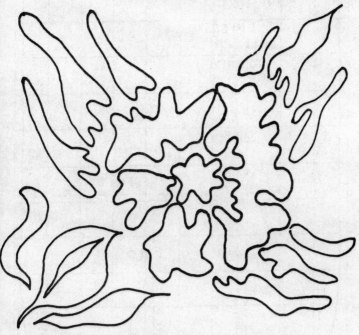

5. Tear the backing paper off the Bondaweb and iron the pieces on to one of the flaps and front panel of the oval bag.

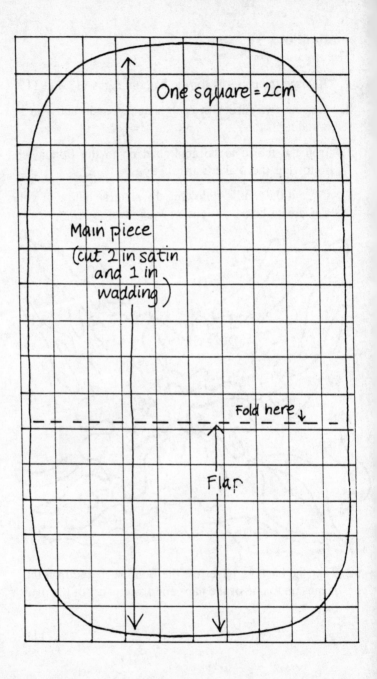

One square = 2cm

Main piece
(cut 2 in satin
and 1 in
wadding)

Fold here ↓

Flap

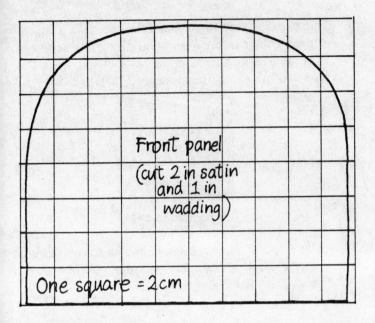

Front panel
(cut 2 in satin
and 1 in
wadding)

One square = 2cm

6. With the satin facing outwards, sandwich the wadding between the two main pieces, and sew all the way round, 5mm from the edge.

7. For the bag front, put the right sides together and wadding underneath and sew along the straight edge of the front panel. Iron the seam and turn the bag right side out.

←Wadding

8. To make bias strip to go round the bag, take a square of main colour material and fold diagonally across to make a triangle. Cut along the fold line as shown to give two pieces of triangle-shaped material.

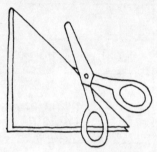

9. Taking one of these triangles, measure a line 2.5cm from the diagonal and mark with pins. Cut along this line as shown.

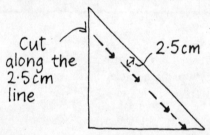

Cut along the 2.5cm line

2.5cm

10. Repeat step 9 with the other triangle and join the two strips along their short diagonal edges at right angles to each other as shown.

11. Pin, catching the cord strap in the side seams, then, around the curved edge, sew the front panel to the back of the bag with the inside lining together.

12. Sew bias binding all the way round the bag.

13. Sew a press stud on to the flap and front panel.

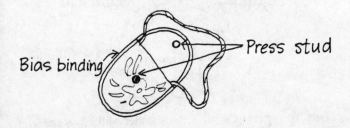

For a circular bag

1. For a circular bag, draw round a small tea plate to make your pattern. Cut four white satin circles, and two slightly smaller wadding circles.

2. Iron the black satin fabric to be appliquéd on to the Bondaweb following the maker's instructions and cut out some motifs of your own design.

3. Iron the black motifs on to one of the white satin circles.

4. With right sides together sew the front to the back

round two-thirds of the bag as shown. Turn it the right side out and press. Do the same with the two lining circles leaving the right sides together. Press.

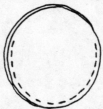

5. Place the lining circles into the outer circles, and slip the wadding in between the two layers on each side of the bag.

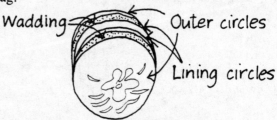

6. Turn the opening's raw-edges under and close the gap between the outer and inner bag back and front by slip stitching. Sew a press stud near the top-edge of the inside front and back of the bag.

7. Sew a circle of braid about two-thirds of the way round the bag, and continue to make a handle.

●●● Victorian Gift Cushions

These decorative, pretty pin
cushions are an unusual gift to give
for a special occasion. The main
part of the design is worked in pins, so *never* give a
cushion to a baby or young child to play with. It is a keep-
sake to be treasured and perhaps passed on from one
generation to the next.

If you have some old bits of lace or silk or some fine
ribbons, they can be incorporated into the design. The
cushions can be given as Christmas, christening, Valen-
tine, wedding or engagement presents. You can create any
design you want but it is a good idea to use pale coloured
fabrics for the actual cushion as this brings out the colours
and detail of your pin design.

You will need

Scissors
Needle and thread
24cm of silk, satin, velvet or any other beautiful fabric.
24cm of close-woven lining fabric (this is enough fabric to
    make six 10cm × 13cm cushions)
Sawdust or bran for filling (buy this from pet shops)
108cm of 1–2cm wide lace or narrow ribbon per cushion.
Rust proof pins, with assorted colour heads
Graph paper
Sharp pencil
Thin tissue paper

117

Instructions

1. Cut out two pieces of lining fabric and two pieces of top fabric for each cushion (12cm × 15cm). Use a 1cm seam allowance.

2. To make the cushion pad, sew together with the wrong sides out the two pieces of lining fabric around three and a half sides. Turn the fabric the right side out, fill with bran and close the gap by oversewing.

3. Make the cover in the same way as you have the lining but leave one side unsewn, and use a slightly larger seam allowance. Turn the cover the right side out and put it over the cushion pad — it should be a tight fit. Close the open side by oversewing.

4. Work out your design for the cushion on graph paper as you would a tapestry design, allowing one square for one pin head.

5. Place the tissue paper over the design you have drawn and carefully trace it.

6. Secure the tissue paper over one side of the cushion and, following your pencil guide lines, pin through the paper on to the cushion to make your design.

7. Very gently pull away the paper. This is a fiddly job so be patient.

8. Sew the lace or ribbon around the edge of the cushion by hand. Place a few pins along each side of this border.

Food Presents

Everyone has to eat, so you can make an edible present to suit the taste of the recipient. If you are a good cook here is a wonderful opportunity to use your skills.

●●● Green Tomato Chutney

You will need

1 kilo (2 lbs) green tomatoes
200g (8oz) onions
200g (8oz) apples
150ml (¼ pint) malt vinegar
100g (4oz) sultanas
1 teaspoon salt
½ teaspoon cayenne pepper
½ teaspoon dry mustard
200g (8oz) sugar

Equipment

Fork
Sharp knife
Steel or aluminium saucepan
Wooden spoon
Warm, dry, clean jam jars
Wax and cellophane lids
Elastic bands
Labels
Pen

119

Instructions

1. Skin the tomatoes before using them. To do this stick a fork into them, plunge them into boiling water for a few seconds, then take them out and peel off the skin.

2. Chop the skinned tomatoes and put them in the pan.

3. Peel and chop the onions and add them to the pan.

4. Peel, core and chop the apples and add them to the pan.

5. Add about half the vinegar and cook gently until the tomatoes and apples are soft, stirring well all the time.

6. Add the rest of the vinegar and the other ingredients and continue to cook steadily until the chutney thickens. This should take about fifteen minutes.

7. Pour the chutney into clean jam jars and seal them tightly with wax lids and elastic bands. Label the jars while the chutney is still slightly runny.

●●● Tomato Ketchup

Freshly-made ketchup is much
nicer than the shop-bought variety.

You will need

3 kilos (6lbs) red tomatoes
1 onion
3 cloves of garlic
1 teaspoon paprika
1 teaspoon cayenne pepper
Juice of 1 orange
1 teaspoon salt
200g (8oz) white sugar
300ml (½ pint) white vinegar

Equipment

Sharp knife
Saucepan
Wooden spoon
Sieve
Bowl
Funnel
Bottles or jars (old ketchup bottles with screw lids are
   ideal, but they must be washed and sterilized)
Labels

Instructions

1. Peel and chop the tomatoes and put them in the pan.

121

2. Peel and chop the onion and garlic and add these to the pan.

3. Cook slowly, stirring all the time, until the onions are soft and the tomatoes pulpy.

4. Add all the other ingredients and continue cooking until the mixture has a thick, even consistency.

5. Sieve the mixture into a bowl until you have smooth lump-free ketchup. (Note: the ketchup will thicken on cooling.)

6. Pour the ketchup through the funnel into the sterilized bottles. Put on the lids.

7. Label the bottles.

This ketchup must be kept in the fridge once it has been opened.

●●● Hot Spicy Nuts

You will need

250g (10oz) unblanched whole almonds
1 tablespoon chilli powder (this is very hot — if you prefer
    something less spicy, use paprika)
1 large clove of garlic
50g (2oz) butter, chopped
Coarse salt

Equipment

Heavy-bottomed frying pan
Wooden spoon
Airtight jar

Instructions

1. Peel and crush the garlic and put it in the frying pan.

2. Add the chilli or paprika, butter, salt and nuts.

3. Toss the mixture over a medium heat until the nuts
    become crisp and light brown.

4. Sprinkle them with salt and allow them to cool.

●●● Lemon Curd

This is yummy but it doesn't keep for long. It is important to thicken the curd very slowly, without

boiling, or else it may curdle. If this does happen, remove the mixture from the heat and whisk it vigorously.

You will need

3 lemons
3 eggs
175g (7oz) sugar
50g (2oz) butter

Equipment

Lemon grater
Either a double saucepan *or* a saucepan with a bowl that fits snugly into it, so the rim of the bowl rests on the edge of the saucepan
Lemon squeezer
Sharp knife
Wooden spoon
Cup
Sterilized, warm jars
Labels

Makes approximately 450ml (¾ pint)

Instructions

1. Grate the rind of the lemons so that only the zest (yellow) is removed. Put this into the top saucepan of

a double saucepan, or bowl if using a saucepan and bowl.

2. Cut the lemons in half, squeeze them, and add the juice to the rind.

3. Heat up the water in the saucepan (the lower one if using a double saucepan).

4. Break the eggs into a cup and beat them.

5. Add the sugar and butter to the ingredients in the bowl or saucepan. Simmer the mixture until the sugar dissolves.

6. Turn the heat down low, add the eggs and stir until the mixture thickens.

7. Pour the mixture into the sterilized jars and label them.

8. Allow the jars to cool before storing them in the fridge, or giving them as presents.

●●● Florentines

These are luxurious chocolatey
fruity biscuits.

You will need

50g (2oz) unsalted butter
50g (2oz) brown sugar
2 tablespoons plain flour
25g (1oz) finely chopped walnuts
25g (1oz) sliced almonds
25g (1oz) finely chopped hazelnuts
1 tablespoon finely chopped glacé cherries
2 tablespoons finely chopped mixed candied peel
100g (4oz) plain chocolate
1 teaspoon margarine

FLORENTISSIMO!

Equipment

Baking trays
Mixing bowl
Wooden spoon
Tablespoon
Wire rack
Airtight tin
Either a double saucepan *or* a bowl and saucepan (see
    p. 124, Lemon curd)
Palette knife
Fork

Instructions

1. Turn the oven on to 180°C/350°F/Gas Mark 4, and

grease the baking trays.

2. Cream the butter and sugar together until the mixture is light and fluffy.

3. Mix the flour, and stir in the nuts, cherries and candied peel.

4. Using a tablespoon, spoon the mixture on to the baking trays leaving a gap of 10cm between each biscuit, as the mixture spreads when it cooks.

5. Bake for four minutes or until the biscuits are golden brown in colour.

6. Remove the trays from the oven. Allow them to cool for one minute and then remove the biscuits with the palette knife and put them on a wire rack to cool.

7. Slowly melt the chocolate and margarine in the top saucepan of a double saucepan or in a basin over a pan of very hot water.

8. Spread the chocolate on to the underside of each biscuit in turn, mark with a fork pattern as shown.

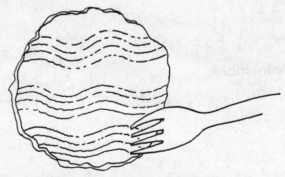

9. Put the biscuits in the fridge to set.

10. Store them in an airtight tin.

● Marzipan Fruits

Real marzipan made from ground
almonds is lovely and tastes
nothing like bought marzipan.

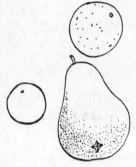

You will need

100g (4oz) finely ground almonds
100g (4oz) icing sugar
1 egg white
Red, blue, yellow and green food colouring
Cloves

Equipment

Bowl
Wooden spoon
Clean dry cloth
Fine artist's paintbrushes
Saucer
Paper cases for sweets
Box

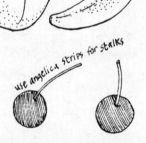

use angelica strips for stalks

Instructions

1. Mix the almonds, sugar, and egg white together in a
   bowl.

2. On a table, knead the mixture together until it becomes
   a smooth dry paste.

3. Roll the mixture into a ball, cover it with a cloth and
   leave it to stand for fifteen minutes.

4. Break off pieces of the marzipan about the size of a walnut and roll them into the fruit shapes you want — banana, orange, melon, pear, grapes etc.

5. Paint on the colour of your fruit. For orange, mix yellow and red food colouring together in a saucer. For green, mix blue with yellow. For purple, a mixture of blue and red is needed.

6. Stick cloves into the oranges, apples and pears, to make stems.

7. Place the fruits in little paper cases and put them in a pretty box.

●●● Cherry and Walnut Shortbread

You will need

200g (8oz) butter (use at room temperature)
87.5g (3½oz) castor sugar
225g (9oz) plain flour
60g (2oz) ground rice
25g (1oz) cherries
25g (1oz) chopped walnuts

Equipment

Bowl
Wooden spoon
Baking tin
Knife
Wire rack

Instructions

1. Turn the oven on to 150°C/300°F/Gas Mark 2.

2. Cream together the butter and sugar.

3. Add the flour and ground rice. (If the mixture is too heavy to move with a spoon, use your VERY CLEAN hands.)

4. Add the cherries and nuts.

5. Gently press the mixture into a baking tin to a thickness of about 5mm.

130

6. Bake for about one hour or until the shortbread is golden brown.

7. Remove the tray from the oven and mark the segments with a knife before the shortbread cools.

8. Leave the shortbread for a minute before turning it out on to a wire rack to cool.

● Stuffed Dates

These are a very good present to
give at Christmas

You will need

125g (5oz) block of marzipan (or make your own,
  see p. 128)
Box of dates
Caster sugar
Paper cases for sweets
Pretty tin or box

Instructions

1. Divide the marzipan into twenty pieces and roll each
   piece so it looks like a small sausage.

2. Remove the stones from the dates.

3. Place a piece of marzipan in each date.

4. Roll each stuffed date in caster sugar.

5. Put each stuffed date into a paper case and then inside
   the tin or box.

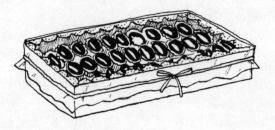

Growing Presents

People who are good at growing things are said to have green fingers — perhaps you are one of these fortunate people. However, even if you aren't, here are a few easy presents you can make.

● Mustard and Cress

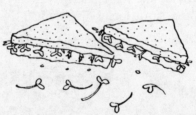

You will need

A box (a seed box, or an old shoe box with the sides cut down will do)
Some earth
Water
Cress seed
Newspaper
Mustard seed

Instructions

1. Put some earth in the box so that the bottom is covered, and wet it well.

2. Sprinkle on some cress seed and then cover the box with newspaper.

3. Four days later add a sprinkling of mustard seed (mustard germinates quicker than cress). Cover the box with newspaper again.

133

4. Keep checking the seeds to see when the plants appear. As soon as they do, remove the newspaper and expose them to the light, by placing your box on a window sill.

5. Either give the seedlings as they are or cut them with scissors when they are a few inches high to make delicious sandwiches.

●● Tomatoes

Tomatoes are a lovely present to
give as nothing tastes quite as
sweet as fresh tomatoes. If you
have too many, make tomato ketchup (see p. 121). If the
tomatoes don't ripen, make green tomato chutney
(see p. 119).

Tomatoes need a fairly mild climate and some sun. They
are best grown against a south-facing wall. You can grow
tomatoes from seed, if you are an inexperienced gardener
it is best to buy seedlings from your local nursery at the
end of May or early June.

You will need

Tomato plants
A patch of ground *or* a Gro bag
Trowel
Bamboo canes
Lots of water

Instructions

1. At the end of May or the beginning of June, buy your
    seedlings from a nursery. (If you are going to use a
    Gro bag, buy this at the same time.) Buy three or four
    plants for a Gro bag.

2. Using a trowel, make holes in the soil, or Gro bag,
    50cm apart.

3. Gently turn each pot upside down, hold your hand

over the soil, and shake hard. The plant, surrounded by soil, should come out in your hand.

4. Carefully lower the plant with its soil into the hole.

5. Fill any gaps with earth and then press down on the soil so that the plant is firm.

6. Water well, and stick a bamboo cane in the ground or Gro bag for the tomato to grow up. As the plant grows you will need to tie it to the stake to stop it falling over.

7. Pick off the side shoots as the plant grows. When there are four trusses of flowers on the plant, break off the top to stop the plant getting any higher.

8. Remember to keep the tomatoes well watered. Put the water on the ground *not* on the plant.

● Radishes

Grow these outside between
February and the beginning of
August. Allow six weeks' growing
time.

You will need

Patch of garden
Rake
Trowel
Radish seeds

Instructions

1. Make sure your piece of ground is free of weeds and stones. Rake it well so that there are no large lumps of earth.

2. Make a shallow drill or small furrow using your trowel.

3. Put the seeds in the drill 20cm apart.

4. Cover the seeds with soil and rake over.

The radishes will be ready to eat six weeks later.

Note: radishes need lots of water so, if it doesn't rain much, remember to water them.

Beauty Presents

Because you are the maker of these magic potions, you know that your products are kind to skin. However, because they are preservative-free, it means that they will only stay fresh for about two weeks and they must be stored in an airtight container in the fridge. Remember you must be scrupulously clean when making beauty products so as to avoid contamination.

Collect pretty jars with screw top lids, and use these to store your potions in.

Most of the recipes are ●●● as they involve the use of an electric blender. So ask an adult's permission before starting and do be very careful.

● Yoghurt and Yeast Face Mask

This is particularly good for dry skin.

You will need

3 teaspoonfuls lemon juice
3 tablespoons of natural yoghurt
3 tablespoons of powdered brewer's yeast (available from chemists)
3 teaspoonfuls olive oil

Equipment

Sharp knife
Lemon squeezer
Mixing bowl
Wooden spoon
Plastic funnel
Clean, dry jar with lid for storing
Label
Pen

Instructions

1. Cut the lemon in half and squeeze out the juice.

2. Measure out three teaspoonfuls of the juice and put it into the mixing bowl, together with all the other ingredients.

3. Mix all the ingredients together well and then pour the mixture through the funnel into a clean, dry jar.

4. Label the jar with the ingredients, the date it was made, and the 'use by' date.

●●● Apple Face Mask

This is a lovely-smelling mask for normal skin.

You will need

Large juicy apple
2 tablespoons thin honey
½ teaspoon sage

Equipment

Apple peeler
A blender
Clean dry jar
Label
Pen

Instructions

1. Peel and core the apple.

2. Place all the ingredients in the blender and whizz for 30 seconds.

3. Check that the ingredients are blended and then pour the mixture into a clean, dry jar.

4. Label the jar with the ingredients, the date it was made and the 'use by' date.

● Hand Cream

You will need

3 tablespoons honey
6 tablespoons almond oil

Equipment

Mixing bowl
Wooden spoon
Plastic funnel
Clean, dry jar with screw-on lid
Label
Pen

Instructions

1. Mix the ingredients together in the bowl.

2. Pour the mixture through the funnel into the clean dry jar.

3. Write on the label the ingredients, the date of making, plus the 'use by' date, and then stick the label on to the jar.

● Hair Rinses

These rinses are for different
coloured hair. Use them after your
normal shampoo.

For brown hair

You will need

Bowl
2 stems of fresh nettles
1 pint of boiling water
Sieve
Clean glass bottle for storage
Label
Pen

Instructions

1. Pour the water into the bowl.

2. Add the nettles and leave them to stand for an hour.

3. Strain the liquid into the bottle.

4. Write a label for the bottle.

For fair or blond hair

You will need

Juice of one lemon
1 pint of water
Clean, dry bottle for storing

142

Label
Pen

Instructions

1. Squeeze the lemon juice into the water.
2. Pour into the bottle and label.

For dark hair

You will need

½ pint of beer
½ pint of water
Label
Pen

Instructions

1. Mix the beer and the water.
2. Pour into the bottle and label.

Wrapping Presents

Sometimes the wrapping paper can cost more than the present, so why not make your own? Below are a few ideas.

1. Use embossed wallpaper and decorate the raised pattern by rubbing it with a wax crayon.

2. Draw a simple pattern on to plain paper using a glue stick and then sprinkle it with glitter. Shake off any excess glitter and tip it back into the container.

3. Mix up water colour paint and then dip a sponge into it and cover the paper with sponge marks. Mix up another colour and sponge over the first colour.

4. Cut up paper doilies and stick them all over a plain background for a lacy gift wrap.

5. Make a cube-shaped present into a dice by covering it in black paper and sticking on white dots. Or make a domino from an oblong present such as a board game.

6. If you have a very awkward-shaped present, wrap it in cellophane as this doesn't crumple like ordinary paper.